THE KITCHEN LIBRARY

PARTY COOKING

THE KITCHEN LIBRARY

PARTY COOKING

Norma MacMillan

OCTOPUS BOOKS

CONTENTS

This edition published 1989 by
Octopus Books Limited
a division of the Octopus Publishing Group
Michelin House
81 Fulham Road
London SW3 6RB

ISBN 0 7064 3842 6

Printed by Mandarin Offset in Hong Kong

INTRODUCTION

When friends or family get together, whether 4 or 24 guests, you have a party to cater for. It could be an intimate dinner with close friends, a Christmas family reunion or a riotous child's birthday party.

This summer why not have some friends over for a back garden barbecue? Or enjoy a picnic – if the weather permits? Or provide sumptuous buffet fare for a crowd of friends. Whatever the event, *The Pick 'n Pay Book of Party Cooking* will give you new and exciting cookery ideas.

You will find recipes from all over the world that can be exotic, sophisticated or just plain delicious. And many can be prepared in advance so that you can escape the kitchen and enjoy the party as much as your guests.

NOTES

Standard spoon measurements are used in all recipes
1 teaspoon = one 5 ml spoon
1 tablespoon = one 15 ml spoon
All spoon measures are level.

Fresh herbs are used unless otherwise stated. If unobtainable substitute a bouquet garni of the equivalent dried herbs, or use dried herbs instead but halve the quantities stated.
Freshly ground black pepper should be used unless white pepper is specified.

Ovens should be preheated to the specified temperature.

For all recipes, quantities are given in both metric and imperial measures. Follow either set of measures but not a mixture of both, because they are not interchangeable.

Avocado with Crab

1 large avocado, peeled, stoned and cubed
350 g (12 oz) fresh or canned crabmeat, flaked
2 celery sticks, diced
6 radishes, sliced
4 spring onions, finely chopped
3 tablespoons tarragon vinegar
3 tablespoons lemon juice
salt and pepper
few lettuce leaves
8 tablespoons mayonnaise
2 tablespoons tomato purée

Mix together the avocado, crabmeat, celery, radishes, spring onions, vinegar, lemon juice and salt and pepper to taste. Line 6 small glass dishes with lettuce leaves and pile the avocado mixture on top.

Mix together the mayonnaise and tomato purée, then spoon a little of this dressing on top of each salad.

Serves 6

Orange and Grapefruit Cups

3 large grapefruit
2 oranges
2 tablespoons medium sherry
6 mint sprigs (if available)

Halve the grapefruit, loosen the segments with a serrated grapefruit knife and place in a bowl. Scrape out the grapefruit shells to remove all the membrane, then set aside. Add any residual juice to the segments.

Remove the orange segments in the same way, but do not bother to clean the orange shells – just squeeze the juice from them and add to the orange and grapefruit segments with the sherry.

Pile into the grapefruit shells. Garnish each with a mint sprig and serve chilled.

Serves 6

Grilled Sprats with Lemon Butter

500 g (1 lb) sprats
salt
cayenne pepper
125 g (4 oz) butter
juice of 1 lemon
lemon slice and watercress to garnish

Clean the sprats through the gills, then rinse under cold water and pat dry. Arrange the sprats on the grill rack, in one layer, and sprinkle with salt and cayenne. Grill for about 3 minutes on each side.

Meanwhile, melt the butter in a saucepan. Stir in the lemon juice.

Arrange the sprats on a large warmed serving dish and sprinkle with the lemon butter. Garnish with the lemon slice and watercress, and serve with brown bread and butter.

Serves 4

Olive Stuffed Eggs

24 large black olives, stoned
6 hard-boiled eggs
25 g (1 oz) butter, softened
salt and pepper
milk (as necessary)
watercress

Cut one of the olives into thin slices and reserve for garnish if wished. Purée the remaining olives in an electric blender.

Halve the eggs and remove the yolks. Mix the yolks with the olive purée, butter and salt and pepper to taste to make a smooth, evenly blended mixture. If it is too thick, add a little milk.

Spoon or pipe the mixture into the egg whites and garnish each with an olive slice. Serve on a bed of watercress.

Serves 6

Lettuce and Bacon Salad

250 g (8 oz) unsmoked streaky bacon rashers, derinded and diced
8 spring onions, finely chopped
4 tablespoons red wine vinegar
4 tablespoons water
4 teaspoons sugar
salt and pepper
2 large soft-leaved cabbage lettuces
6 radishes, thinly sliced
1 hard-boiled egg, finely chopped

Fry the bacon in a dry frying pan until it is crisp and has rendered its fat. Remove with a slotted spoon.

Add the spring onions to the pan and fry until softened. Stir in the vinegar, water, sugar, bacon and salt and pepper to taste. Bring to the boil, stirring.

Tear the lettuce into small pieces and place in a salad bowl. Pour over the hot dressing and toss well. Garnish with the radishes and sprinkle the egg on top. Serve immediately.

Serves 6

Pâté Maison

500 g (1 lb) minced veal
750 g (1½ lb) minced pork
2 cloves garlic, halved
2 large onions, sliced
175 ml (6 fl oz) dry white wine
2 tablespoons brandy
2 tablespoons oil
salt and pepper
350 g (12 oz) streaky bacon rashers, derinded

Mix together the veal and pork in a bowl. Sprinkle the garlic and onion on top and pour over the wine, brandy and oil. Cover and leave to marinate overnight.

Discard the onion. Crush the garlic and stir into the meat mixture with the liquid. Add salt and pepper to taste.

Stretch the bacon rashers with the back of a knife and use all but 4 of them to line a 1 kg (2 lb) loaf tin. Spoon in the meat mixture and smooth the top. Cover with the remaining bacon rashers.

Cover the tin with foil and place in a roasting pan containing about 2.5 cm (1 inch) of boiling water. Cook in a preheated moderately hot oven, 190°C (375°F), Gas Mark 5, for 2 hours or until the pâté has shrunk slightly from the sides of the tin, and there is no trace of pink in the juices.

Allow the pâté to cool to room temperature, then put a plate and a weight on top. Chill overnight.

Serves 8 to 10

Prawns in Wine

250 g (8 oz) frozen shelled prawns, thawed
6 tablespoons dry white wine
25 g (1 oz) butter
1 clove garlic, crushed
2 tablespoons dry sherry
salt
25 g (1 oz) Parmesan cheese, grated
175 g (6 oz) long-grain rice
chopped parsley to garnish

Put the prawns in a dish and sprinkle with the wine. Leave to marinate for 2 hours, stirring occasionally.

Melt the butter in a frying pan. Add the garlic and fry until softened, then stir in the prawns and wine, sherry and salt to taste. Cook gently for 10 minutes or until heated through. Stir in the cheese.

Meanwhile, cook the rice in boiling salted water for 10 to 12 minutes until tender. Arrange on 4 warmed serving plates. Pile the prawns on top and garnish with parsley.

Serves 4

Stuffed Mushrooms

24 large flat mushrooms
125 g (4 oz) butter
1 clove garlic, crushed
50 g (2 oz) fresh breadcrumbs
50 g (2 oz) Parmesan cheese, grated
2 tablespoons chopped parsley
salt and pepper

Remove the stems from the mushrooms and chop them finely. Melt half the butter in a frying pan. Add the chopped mushroom stems and garlic and fry until softened. Stir in the breadcrumbs, cheese, parsley and salt and pepper to taste. Remove from the heat.

Melt the remaining butter and pour half into a shallow baking dish. Arrange the mushroom caps in the dish, rounded sides down. Fill each with the cheese mixture and drizzle over the remaining melted butter.

Bake in a preheated moderate oven, 180°C (350°F), Gas Mark 4, for about 15 minutes or until the mushrooms are tender and the stuffing golden.

Serves 6

Celery with Spicy Dressing

3 celery hearts, about 5 cm (2 inches) in diameter
salt and pepper
150 ml (¼ pint) fresh sour cream
4 tablespoons tomato ketchup
4 tablespoons tomato chutney
1½ teaspoons Worcestershire sauce
1 teaspoon horseradish sauce
few drops of Tabasco sauce
few lettuce leaves
TO GARNISH:
2 hard-boiled eggs, sliced
2 spring onions, finely chopped

Trim the celery hearts to about 15 cm (6 inches) long and cut each in half lengthways. Place in a saucepan, add boiling salted water to cover and simmer for 6 to 8 minutes or until just tender. Drain, then plunge into cold water and drain again. Chill.

Mix together the sour cream, ketchup, chutney, Worcestershire sauce, horseradish sauce, Tabasco and salt and pepper to taste. Chill.

Make a bed of lettuce on a serving dish. Place the celery hearts on top and garnish with the egg slices, spring onions and a little dressing. Serve the remaining dressing separately.

Serves 6

Carrot and Parsnip Soup

25 g (1 oz) butter
1 kg (2 lb) carrots, chopped
500 g (1 lb) parsnips, cored and chopped
1 large onion, chopped
2 x 411 g (14½ oz) cans consommé
grated nutmeg
salt and pepper
150 ml (¼ pint) milk or single cream
croûtons to garnish

Melt the butter in a saucepan. Add the carrots, parsnips and onion and fry, stirring occasionally, for 10 minutes. Add the consommé and bring to the boil. Cover and simmer for 30 minutes or until the vegetables are very tender.

Allow to cool slightly, then purée the soup in an electric blender or rub through a sieve. Return to the saucepan and season to taste with nutmeg, salt and pepper. Bring to the boil, stirring then remove from the heat and stir in the milk or cream.

Serve at once, garnished with croûtons.

Serves 6 to 8

Tomato Wine Soup

50 g (2 oz) butter
750 g (1½ lb) tomatoes, skinned, seeded and chopped
3 tablespoons plain flour
large pinch of grated nutmeg
large pinch of dried basil
salt and pepper
300 ml (½ pint) top of the milk or single cream
¼ teaspoon bicarbonate of soda
300 ml (½ pint) dry white wine
chopped parsley to garnish

Melt the butter in a saucepan. Add the tomatoes and cook gently for 5 minutes. Purée the soup in an electric blender or rub through a sieve, then return to the saucepan. Stir in the flour, nutmeg, basil and salt and pepper to taste. Bring to the boil, stirring, and simmer for 2 minutes.

Add the milk or cream and bicarbonate of soda and cook gently, stirring, until very slightly thickened. Stir in the wine and heat through. Serve garnished with parsley.

Serves 6

NOTE: Use tomatoes with plenty of flavour for this soup.

Velvety Chicken Soup

75 g (3 oz) butter
40 g (1½ oz) plain flour
750 ml (1¼ pints) homemade chicken stock
150 ml (¼ pint) milk
150 ml (¼ pint) single cream
250 g (8 oz) cooked chicken meat, finely chopped
salt and pepper

Melt the butter in a saucepan. Add the flour and cook, stirring, for 2 minutes. Gradually stir in the stock and bring to the boil, stirring. Simmer for 5 minutes.

Add the milk, cream, chicken and salt and pepper to taste and stir well. Heat through gently before serving.
Serves 6

Hearty Fish Soup

2 tablespoons oil
1 large onion, chopped
1 clove garlic, crushed
3 celery sticks, diced
2 x 397 g (14 oz) cans tomatoes
900 ml (1½ pints) fish or chicken stock
¼ teaspoon dried oregano
¼ teaspoon dried basil
¼ teaspoon dried rosemary
65 g (2½ oz) long-grain rice
250 g (8 oz) sliced green beans
750 g (1½ lb) cod or halibut fillets, cut into cubes
salt and pepper
2 tablespoons chopped parsley

Heat the oil in a saucepan. Add the onion, garlic and celery and fry until softened. Stir in the tomatoes with their juice, stock, herbs and rice. Bring to the boil, then cover and simmer for 10 minutes.

Add the beans and continue simmering, covered, until the rice is tender. Add the fish and simmer for 5 minutes or until the fish is tender. Adjust the seasoning and sprinkle with parsley.

Serves 6 to 8

Sweetcorn and Chicken Soup

25 g (1 oz) butter
1 onion, finely chopped
1 green pepper, cored, seeded and diced
15 g (½ oz) flour
600 ml (1 pint) home-made chicken stock
3 medium potatoes, cooked and diced
125 g (4 oz) cooked chicken meat, chopped
1 x 326 g (11½ oz) can sweetcorn kernels, drained
salt and pepper
150 ml (¼ pint) milk or single cream

Melt the butter in a saucepan. Add the onion and green pepper and fry until softened. Stir in the flour and cook for 2 minutes, then gradually stir in the stock. Bring to the boil and simmer, stirring frequently, for 5 minutes.

Add the potatoes, chicken and sweetcorn and cook gently for 10 minutes or until the ingredients are heated through. Add salt and pepper to taste, then stir in the milk or cream. Serve hot.

Serves 6

Iced Crème Courgette

25 g (1 oz) butter
500 g (1 lb) courgettes, thinly sliced
750 ml (1¼ pints) chicken stock
salt and pepper
¼ teaspoon dried Italian herbs
½ bunch of watercress, stalks removed
150 ml (¼ pint) fresh sour cream
3 ice cubes, crushed

Melt the butter in a saucepan. Add the courgettes and cook gently until tender. Stir in the stock, salt and pepper to taste and herbs. Reserve a few watercress sprigs for garnish and add the rest to the pan. Bring to the boil, then cover and simmer gently for 20 minutes.

Purée the soup in an electric blender or rub through a sieve, then pour into a bowl. Cool, then cover and chill thoroughly.

Just before serving, stir in the sour cream. Serve garnished with crushed ice and the reserved watercress sprigs.

Serves 6

NOTE: To crush ice, place the ice cubes in a polythene bag and beat with a rolling pin.

Chilled Spring Vegetable Soup

250 g (8 oz) carrots, diced
250 g (8 oz) leeks, thinly sliced
350 g (12 oz) new potatoes, diced
900 ml (1½ pints) chicken stock
1 bunch of watercress, stalks trimmed
150 ml (¼ pint) milk
grated nutmeg
salt and pepper
2 streaky bacon rashers, derinded and diced
3 spring onions, finely chopped

Put the carrots, leeks, potatoes and stock in a saucepan and bring to the boil. Cover and simmer for 15 minutes or until the vegetables are tender.

Stir in the watercress and cook for 2 minutes. Purée the soup in an electric blender or rub through a sieve, then pour into a bowl. Add the milk and season to taste with nutmeg, salt and pepper. Cool, then cover and chill thoroughly.

Meanwhile, fry the bacon in its own fat until crisp. Drain on kitchen paper. Serve the chilled soup garnished with the bacon and spring onions.

Serves 6

Baked Marinated Halibut

6 halibut steaks
6 tablespoons oil
3 tablespoons lemon juice
2 teaspoons Moutarde de Meaux
salt and pepper
25 g (1 oz) butter
1 onion, finely chopped
50 g (2 oz) fresh breadcrumbs
25 g (1 oz) Parmesan cheese, grated
2 tablespoons chopped parsley

Arrange the halibut steaks in a dish in one layer. Mix together the oil, lemon juice, Meaux mustard and salt and pepper to taste and pour over the fish. Leave to marinate for at least 30 minutes, turning occasionally.

Drain the fish steaks and arrange in a baking dish in one layer. Melt the butter in a frying pan. Add the onion and fry until softened. Stir in the breadcrumbs, cheese and parsley. Spread this mixture over the fish steaks. Bake in a preheated moderate oven, 180°C (350°F), Gas Mark 4, for 30 minutes or until the fish is cooked.

Serves 6

Plaice Baked in Sour Cream

15 g (½ oz) butter
1.5 kg (3 lb) plaice fillets, skinned and cut into strips
juice of ½ lemon
salt and pepper
1 tablespoon chopped fresh tarragon
450 ml (¾ pint) fresh sour cream
2 teaspoons chopped parsley

Grease a baking dish with the butter. Put the fish strips in the dish and sprinkle with the lemon juice, salt and pepper to taste and the tarragon. Cover with the sour cream.

Bake in a preheated moderate oven, 180°C (350°F), Gas Mark 4, for 25 minutes or until the fish is cooked through. Serve garnished with the parsley.

Serves 6

Fish Steaks with Vermouth

25 g (1 oz) fresh breadcrumbs
salt and pepper
4 salmon steaks
50 g (2 oz) butter
2 teaspoons lemon juice
4 tablespoons dry vermouth
lemon slices and parsley sprig to garnish

Mix the breadcrumbs with salt and pepper and use to coat the fish steaks. Melt the butter in a frying pan. Add the fish steaks and brown on both sides. Transfer the steaks to a baking dish and pour over the butter from the pan. Sprinkle with the lemon juice and vermouth.

Bake in a preheated moderately hot oven, 190°C (375°F), Gas Mark 5, for 15 to 20 minutes. Garnish with the lemon slices and parsley.

Serves 4

Orange Baked Chicken

2 eggs, beaten
6 tablespoons orange juice
50 g (2 oz) fresh breadcrumbs
1½ teaspoons grated orange rind
1 teaspoon paprika
salt and pepper
6 chicken quarters
75 g (3 oz) butter, melted
orange wedges and watercress to garnish

Mix together the eggs and orange juice in a shallow dish. Combine the breadcrumbs, orange rind, paprika and salt and pepper to taste on a sheet of greaseproof paper. Dip the chicken quarters in the egg mixture, then coat with the breadcrumb mixture.

Pour half the melted butter into a roasting pan. Arrange the chicken quarters in the pan in one layer and drizzle over the remaining butter. Bake in a preheated moderately hot oven, 190°C (375°F), Gas Mark 5, for 1 hour or until the chicken is cooked through, turning the chicken quarters halfway through cooking.

Serve garnished with orange wedges and watercress.

Serves 6

Chicken with Tarragon

125 g (4 oz) butter
3 tablespoons chopped tarragon
salt and pepper
1 x 2 kg (4½ lb) oven-ready chicken
1 tablespoon plain flour
170 ml (6 fl oz) double cream
parsley sprigs to garnish

Cream the butter with the tarragon and salt and pepper to taste. Loosen the skin over the breast of the chicken and press in one quarter of the tarragon butter to cover each side of the breast. Form the remaining butter into a ball and place inside the chicken. Truss the bird and place in a roasting pan.

Roast in a preheated moderately hot oven, 190°C (375°F), Gas Mark 5, for 1½ hours or until the chicken is cooked through. Transfer to a heated serving dish and untruss.

Skim off all the clear fat from the juices in the tin. Mix the flour with the cream and stir into the juices. Cook gently on top of the stove, stirring, until thickened. Serve the chicken, garnished with parsley and accompanied by the sauce.

Serves 4 to 6

Chicken Cacciatore

6 or 12 chicken pieces
salt and pepper
50 g (2 oz) butter
3 tablespoons olive oil
1 onion, chopped
2 cloves garlic, crushed
125 g (4 oz) button mushrooms, sliced
150 ml (1/4 pint) dry white wine
4 tablespoons chicken stock
1 x 227 g (8 oz) can tomatoes, drained and chopped
4 tablespoons tomato purée
2 bay leaves
1 teaspoon dried basil
2 tablespoons brandy

Rub the chicken pieces with salt and pepper. Melt the butter with the oil in a flameproof casserole. Add the chicken pieces, in batches, and brown on all sides; remove from the casserole as they brown.

Add the onion and garlic to the casserole and fry until softened. Add the mushrooms and fry for 2 minutes. Stir in the wine, stock, tomatoes, tomato purée, bay leaves and basil and bring to the boil.

Return the chicken pieces to the casserole and simmer, uncovered, for 10 minutes. Cover and continue simmering for 20 minutes or until the chicken is cooked through. Remove the bay leaves and stir in the brandy, adjust the seasoning and serve.

Serves 6

Honey Curry Chicken

75 g (3 oz) butter
175 g (6 oz) clear honey
1 1/2 teaspoons mild curry powder
6 tablespoons German mustard
salt and pepper
8 chicken breasts, skinned

Melt the butter in a saucepan and stir in the honey, curry powder, mustard and salt and pepper to taste. Cook, stirring, until well blended.

Arrange the chicken breasts in a roasting tin in one layer and pour over the honey mixture. Turn the chicken breasts to coat on all sides.

Roast in a preheated moderately hot oven, 190°C (375°F), Gas Mark 5, for 1 hour or until the chicken is cooked through, turning the chicken over halfway through cooking.

Serves 4

Apricot Honey Duckling

1 x 2 kg (4½ lb) oven-ready duckling
300 g (10 oz) apricot jam
150 g (5 oz) clear honey
2 tablespoons brandy
watercress to garnish

Truss the duckling and prick the breast all over. Place on a rack in a roasting pan and roast in a preheated moderate oven, 180°C (350°F), Gas Mark 4, for about 1½ hours or until the duckling is nearly cooked.

Mix together the jam, honey and brandy. Pour off all the fat from the roasting pan and place the duckling in the pan, without the rack. Coat the duckling with the apricot mixture.

Raise the oven temperature to hot, 230°C (450°F), Gas Mark 8, and roast the duckling for a further 10 to 15 minutes or until the glaze caramelizes. Serve garnished with watercress.

Serves 4

Whisky Beef Pot Roast

6 strips pork fat
150 ml (¼ pint) whisky
1 x 1.25 kg (2½ lb) boned beef topside
3 carrots, sliced
1 bouquet garni
450 ml (¾ pint) red wine
¼ teaspoon grated nutmeg
salt and pepper
50 g (2 oz) beef dripping
15 g (½ oz) butter
1 tablespoon plain flour

Soak the strips of fat in the whisky for 1 hour. Drain, reserving the whisky. Insert the strips into the beef using a larding needle. Place in a bowl with the carrots, bouquet garni, whisky, wine, nutmeg and salt and pepper to taste. Cover and leave to marinate overnight.

Drain the beef, reserving the marinade. Melt the dripping in a saucepan or flameproof casserole. Put in the beef and brown on all sides. Pour in the marinade and bring to the boil. Cover and simmer for 2 hours or until the beef is tender. Transfer to a warmed serving dish.

Skim any fat from the cooking liquid, strain and return to the pan. Mix the butter with the flour to make a paste. Add a little of the hot liquid, mix well, then stir into the pan. Simmer, stirring, until thickened.

Serve the beef with the sauce.

Serves 6 to 8

Cranberry Beef Stew

50 g (2 oz) plain flour
1 teaspoon dried basil
salt and pepper
1.25 kg (2½ lb) beef chuck steak, cut into 5 cm (2 inch) cubes
50 g (2 oz) beef dripping or lard (approximately)
300 ml (½ pint) beef stock
6 whole cloves
1 cinnamon stick or ¼ teaspoon ground cinnamon
2 x 184 g (6½ oz) jars cranberry sauce
2 tablespoons lemon juice
15 g (½ oz) butter
parsley sprigs to garnish

Mix the flour with the basil, salt and pepper and use to coat the steak cubes. Reserve any leftover flour. Heat the beef dripping or lard in a frying pan. Add the steak cubes, in batches, and brown on all sides, using more dripping or lard as needed. Transfer the steak cubes to a flameproof casserole as they brown.

Add the stock, cloves and cinnamon to the casserole and bring to the boil. Cover and simmer gently for 2 hours.

Stir in the cranberry sauce and lemon juice. Continue simmering, covered, for 20 to 30 minutes or until the steak cubes are very tender.

Blend the butter with the remaining flour to make a paste. Add a little of the hot liquid from the pan, mix well, then stir into the pan. Simmer, stirring, until slightly thickened. Discard the cinnamon stick if used. Garnish with parsley.

Serves 6

Beef Teriyaki

1.5 kg (3 lb) rump steak
175 ml (6 fl oz) soy sauce
175 ml (6 fl oz) sake or dry sherry
2 tablespoons sugar
1 clove garlic, finely crushed
2 teaspoons finely chopped fresh root ginger or ½ teaspoon ground ginger

Cut the steaks into 5 mm (¼ inch) thick slices. Place between sheets of greaseproof paper and beat with a rolling pin or meat mallet until very thin. Arrange in a large shallow dish or tray.

Mix together the remaining ingredients and pour over the meat. Leave to marinate for at least 1 hour, turning occasionally.

To cook, drain the steak slices and grill for about 1 minute on each side. Serve with rice and stir-fried or steamed vegetables.

Serves 6

NOTE: The teriyaki may also be cooked over charcoal in a barbecue.

Roast Stuffed Leg of Veal

1 x 1.25 kg (2½ lb) boned leg of veal
25 g (1 oz) fresh breadcrumbs
1 teaspoon dried sage
2 tablespoons chopped parsley
1 clove garlic, crushed
3 tablespoons double cream
1 egg yolk
salt and pepper
1 onion, sliced
6 carrots, sliced
1 bay leaf
120 ml (4 fl oz) dry white wine
120 ml (4 fl oz) water
3 tablespoons tomato purée
parsley sprigs to garnish

Lay the veal flat on a working surface. Mix together the breadcrumbs, herbs, garlic, cream, egg yolk, salt and pepper. Spread over the veal, then roll up and tie securely into shape. Rub with salt and pepper and place, join side down, in a roasting tin. Arrange the onion, carrots and bay leaf around the veal.

Roast in a preheated moderately hot oven, 200°C (400°F), Gas Mark 6, for 30 minutes. Turn the veal join side up and continue roasting for 30 minutes.

Turn the veal join side down again. Mix together the wine, water and tomato purée and pour over the meat. Continue roasting, basting frequently, for 1 hour or until the veal is cooked through. If the veal seems to be browning too quickly, cover with foil.

Transfer the veal to a warmed serving dish and garnish with parsley sprigs. Strain the cooking liquid and serve as a sauce.

Serves 6

Veal Olives with Mushrooms

12 small veal escalopes
6 slices of cooked ham
12 spring onions
125 g (4 oz) mature Cheddar cheese, cut into 12 sticks about 5 mm (¼ inch) wide
75 g (3 oz) butter
250 g (8 oz) button mushrooms, sliced
150 ml (¼ pint) dry white wine
salt and pepper
watercress to garnish

Put the escalopes between sheets of greaseproof paper and beat until thin. Cut each slice of ham in half. Place a half ham slice, a spring onion and a stick of cheese on each veal escalope and roll up. Tie with string or secure with wooden cocktail sticks.

Melt the butter in a large frying pan. Add the veal rolls and brown on all sides; remove from the pan as they brown.

Add the mushrooms to the pan and fry for 5 minutes. Stir in the wine with salt and pepper to taste and bring to the boil. Return the veal rolls to the pan and simmer, covered, for about 10 minutes or until the meat is tender. Serve garnished with watercress.

Serves 6

Roast Loin of Pork in White Wine

1 x 1.75 kg (4 lb) loin of pork
4 cloves garlic, cut into slivers
3 parsley sprigs
3 thyme sprigs
1 bay leaf
salt and pepper
4 tablespoons olive oil
450 ml (3/4 pint) dry white wine
fresh herbs to garnish

Make small incisions in the pork around the ribs and bones and insert the garlic slivers. Place in a bowl and add the parsley, thyme, bay leaf and salt and pepper to taste. Pour in the oil and wine. Cover and leave to marinate overnight, turning the meat occasionally.

Transfer the meat to a roasting pan and pour over the marinade. Roast in a preheated moderate oven, 160°C (325°F), Gas Mark 3, for 2½ hours or until the pork is cooked through.

Transfer to a warmed serving dish and keep hot. Skim the fat from the cooking liquid, then strain into a saucepan. Boil to reduce slightly, then adjust the seasoning. Garnish the pork with herbs. Serve the cooking liquid as a sauce.
Serves 6

Pork Fillet with Prunes

175 g (6 oz) prunes, stoned
150 ml (¼ pint) medium sherry
150 ml (¼ pint) water
3 pork fillets
salt and pepper
1½ tablespoons plain flour
170 ml (6 fl oz) double cream
1 tablespoon redcurrant jelly
watercress to garnish

Soak the prunes overnight in the sherry and water; drain, reserving the liquid.

Split open the pork fillets lengthways; do not cut all the way through. Rub the cut surfaces with salt and pepper, then cover with the prunes. Roll up the fillets from the short end and secure with string.

Weigh the rolls and calculate the cooking time, allowing 45 minutes per 500 g (1 lb). Place them in a roasting pan and pour over the reserved prune liquid. Roast in a preheated moderate oven, 180°C (350°F), Gas Mark 4, for the calculated time, or until the pork is cooked through, basting occasionally.

Place the pork rolls on a warmed serving dish and keep hot. Skim any fat from the surface of the cooking liquid. Blend the flour with the cream and stir into the pan juices. Place on top of the stove and cook gently, stirring, until the liquid thickens. Stir in the redcurrant jelly and adjust the seasoning.

Garnish the pork with watercress and serve accompanied by the sauce.

Serves 6

Ginned Lamb Chops

12 lamb chops
50 g (2 oz) butter
4 tablespoons Worcestershire sauce
4 tablespoons lemon juice
4 tablespoons gin
garlic powder
salt and pepper
parsley sprigs to garnish

Arrange the chops in a shallow dish in one layer. Melt the butter in a saucepan. Stir in the remaining ingredients with garlic powder and salt and pepper to taste and pour over the chops. Turn them to coat both sides. Leave to marinate for about 20 minutes.

To cook, drain the chops and grill for 8 to 10 minutes on each side. Serve garnished with parsley.

Serves 6

Illustrated on page 34.

African Curried Lamb

25 g (1 oz) butter
2 tablespoons oil
1.25 kg ($2\frac{1}{2}$ lb) boned lean lamb, cut into 2.5 cm (1 inch) cubes
3 onions, chopped
2 cloves garlic, crushed
4 tablespoons mild curry powder
4 tablespoons cider vinegar
$\frac{1}{2}$ teaspoon paprika
$\frac{1}{4}$ teaspoon cayenne pepper
3 bay leaves
1 x 397 g (14 oz) can tomatoes, chopped
3 tablespoons apricot jam

Melt the butter with the oil in a saucepan. Add the lamb cubes, in batches, and brown on all sides; remove from the pan as they brown.

Add the onions and garlic to the pan and fry until softened. Blend together the curry powder and vinegar and stir into the onions. Cook for 1 minute.

Return the lamb cubes to the pan with the remaining ingredients, including the juice from the tomatoes. Mix well, then cover and simmer for 2 hours or until the lamb is tender.

Uncover the pan and boil rapidly until the liquid has reduced slightly. Discard the bay leaves. Serve with chopped green pepper, tomato wedges, banana slices and chutney.
Serves 6

Lemon-Pear Pork Chops

5 tablespoons oil
6 pork chops
1 onion, chopped
150 ml (¼ pint) orange juice
salt and pepper
3 firm pears, peeled, cored and halved
2 tablespoons brown sugar
6 thin lemon slices
whole cloves
2 teaspoons cornflour

Heat the oil in a frying pan. Add the chops and brown on both sides. Arrange in a baking dish, in one layer.

Add the onion to the pan and fry until softened. Spoon around the chops and pour over the orange juice. Add salt and pepper to taste. Cover and cook in a preheated moderately hot oven, 190°C (375°F), Gas Mark 5, for 45 to 50 minutes or until the chops are cooked through.

Fill each pear half with a little brown sugar and place a lemon slice on each, securing with cloves. Place a pear on each pork chop and bake, uncovered, for 10 minutes.

Transfer the chops and pears to a warmed serving dish and keep hot. Skim the fat from the cooking liquid and strain into a measuring jug. Make up to 175 ml (6 fl oz) with water and pour into a saucepan. Dissolve the cornflour in a little water and add to the pan. Cook, stirring, until thickened. Pour over the chops before serving.

Serves 6

Bananas Baked with Almonds and Rum

8 large bananas
1 tablespoon sugar
120 ml (4 fl oz) white rum
284 ml (10 fl oz) double cream
250 g (8 oz) macaroons, crushed
25 g (1 oz) blanched almonds, chopped
15 g (½ oz) butter, melted

Cut the bananas in half lengthways, then each half in half crossways. Place the pieces in a baking dish and sprinkle with the sugar and rum. Bake in a preheated moderate oven, 160°C (325°F), Gas Mark 3, for 15 minutes.

Pour the cream over the bananas. Mix together the macaroons and almonds and sprinkle over the top. Drizzle with the butter.

Return to the oven and bake for 20 minutes. Serve hot.

Serves 6 to 8

Fruit Brûlée

3 tablespoons sugar (or to taste)
6 tablespoons water
1 tablespoon lemon juice
750 g-1 kg (1½-2 lb) mixed fruit in season (strawberries, peaches, bananas, apples, pears, grapes, etc.), cored and sliced as necessary
284 ml (10 fl oz) double cream
4 tablespoons dark brown sugar

Dissolve the sugar in the water in a small saucepan. Stir in the lemon juice and remove from the heat.

Put the prepared fruit into a flameproof serving dish and stir in the sugar syrup. Press the fruit down to level the top. Whip the cream until stiff and spread over the fruit. Chill until just before serving.

To serve, sprinkle the cream with the brown sugar and grill until the sugar melts. Serve immediately.

Serves 4 to 6

Orange and Lemon Pancake Gâteau

250 g (8 oz) plain flour
½ teaspoon salt
4 tablespoons icing sugar
2 eggs, beaten
600 ml (1 pint) milk
½ teaspoon vanilla essence
oil for shallow frying
FILLING:
350 g (12 oz) sugar
5 tablespoons cornflour
¼ teaspoon salt
250 ml (8 fl oz) orange juice
6 tablespoons lemon juice
1 teaspoon grated lemon rind
25 g (1 oz) butter
5 egg yolks, beaten

To make the pancakes, sift the flour, salt and half the icing sugar into a bowl. Add the eggs and half the milk with the vanilla essence. Beat until smooth. Gradually beat in the remaining milk.

Lightly grease an 18 cm (7 inch) frying pan and place over high heat. When very hot pour in just enough batter to coat the bottom. Cook until golden brown underneath, then turn the pancake and cook the other side. Repeat with the remaining batter to make about 20 pancakes, stacking them, interleaved with greaseproof paper, as they are cooked; keep warm.

To make the filling, put the sugar, cornflour and salt in a basin over a pan of simmering water. Gradually stir in the orange and lemon juices, then the lemon rind and butter. Heat gently, stirring, for 5 minutes. Cover with foil and continue heating, without stirring, for 10 minutes.

Remove the bowl from the pan and stir in the egg yolks. Return to the heat and cook for a further 2 minutes.

Use the filling to sandwich together the pancakes, stacking them one on top of the other. Cover the gâteau with foil and heat through in a preheated moderate oven, 160°C (325°F), Gas Mark 3, for 15 minutes.

Sprinkle with the remaining icing sugar and serve cut into wedges.

Serves 8 to 10

Apricot and Banana Crumble

175 g (6 oz) dried apricots
6 large bananas, sliced
½ teaspoon ground coriander
175 g (6 oz) plain flour
75 g (3 oz) butter
75 g (3 oz) sugar

Soak the apricots in water to cover for 2 hours. Drain and chop them. Put the apricots and bananas in a baking dish and sprinkle with the coriander.

Sift the flour into a bowl and rub in the butter until the mixture resembles breadcrumbs. Stir in the sugar. Sprinkle this crumble topping over the fruit.

Cook in a preheated moderately hot oven, 200°C (400°F), Gas Mark 6, for 45 minutes or until the topping is golden brown. Serve with cream.
Serves 6

Chocolate Liqueur Mousse

125 g (4 oz) plain chocolate
4 tablespoons water
1-2 tablespoons brandy or orange liqueur
4 eggs, separated
whipped cream to decorate

Put the chocolate and 3 tablespoons of the water in a heavy-based saucepan. Heat gently, stirring, until the chocolate has melted. Remove from the heat and stir in the brandy or liqueur.

Whisk the egg yolks with the rest of the water until pale and frothy. Fold in the chocolate mixture. Whisk the egg whites until stiff and fold in.

Spoon the mousse into individual serving dishes and chill well, preferably overnight. Serve decorated with whipped cream.

Serves 4 to 6

Dried Fruit and Melon Compote

15 dried figs, chopped
15 dried dates, stoned and chopped
50 g (2 oz) blanched hazelnuts
50 g (2 oz) blanched almonds
175 g (6 oz) clear honey
6 tablespoons Kirsch
1 large honeydew melon, halved and seeded

Mix together the figs, dates, nuts, honey and Kirsch in a serving dish. Leave to soak for 3 hours, stirring occasionally.

Cut the melon flesh into balls using a melon baller, or cut into cubes. Add to the fruit mixture and stir well. Chill for about 1 hour before serving, with single cream.

Serves 6

Irish Coffee Soufflé

15 g (½ oz) powdered gelatine
250 ml (8 fl oz) strong black coffee
6 eggs, separated
175 g (6 oz) sugar
150 ml (¼ pint) Irish whiskey
284 ml (10 fl oz) double cream
125 g (4 oz) walnuts, finely chopped
whipped cream and walnut halves to decorate

Lightly grease a 1 litre (2 pint) soufflé dish and tie a band of greaseproof paper around the outside of the dish to extend 5 cm (2 inches) above the rim. Grease the inside of the paper collar.

Dissolve the gelatine in the coffee. Cool slightly. Whisk the egg yolks with the sugar in a basin over a pan of hot water until the mixture is very thick and light. (If using an electric beater, no heat is needed.)

Remove from the heat and gradually whisk in the whiskey and the coffee mixture. Place the bowl in another bowl containing ice cubes and chill, whisking occasionally, until the mixture is the consistency of unbeaten egg white.

Whisk the egg whites until stiff. Whip the cream until thick. Fold the cream into the coffee mixture, followed by the egg whites. Spoon into the prepared soufflé dish. Chill for at least 3 hours or until set.

To serve, remove the paper collar and press the chopped walnuts onto the side. Decorate the top with whirls of cream and walnut halves.

Serves 6 to 8

Illustrated on cover: Orange Soufflé. Prepare as above, using water instead of coffee; replace whiskey with the grated rind and juice of 2 oranges. Decorate to taste.

Hazelnut Meringues with Caramel Sauce

4 egg whites
250 g (8 oz) caster sugar
50 g (2 oz) toasted hazelnuts, very finely chopped
vanilla or chocolate ice cream to serve
SAUCE:
250 g (8 oz) caramels, chopped
284 ml (10 fl oz) double cream

Whisk the egg whites until stiff. Add 4 teaspoons of the sugar and continue beating for 1 minute. Fold in the remaining sugar and the hazelnuts. Spoon or pipe 12 hazelnut meringue shells on baking sheets lined with non-stick paper. Sprinkle with a little extra caster sugar.

Place in a preheated very cool oven, 120°C (250°F), Gas Mark ½, for 1 hour, changing the baking sheets around halfway through the cooking.

Carefully lift the meringues from the baking sheets and press in the soft undersides. Replace on the sheets, undersides up, and return to the oven for a further 20 minutes or until completely dry. Cool.

To make the sauce, put the caramel pieces and cream into a saucepan and heat gently, stirring, until melted. If the sauce is too thick, add a little milk.

To serve, sandwich together pairs of meringue shells with ice cream and spoon over the sauce.

Serves 6

Sultana Meringue Pie

SHORTCRUST PASTRY:
250 g (8 oz) plain flour
pinch of salt
50 g (2 oz) butter
50 g (2 oz) lard
water to mix

FILLING:
175 g (6 oz) sultanas
250 ml (8 fl oz) water
75 g (3 oz) brown sugar
25 g (1 oz) butter
15 g (½ oz) plain flour
2 egg yolks
1 teaspoon grated lemon rind
3 tablespoons lemon juice

MERINGUE:
2 egg whites
¼ teaspoon cream of tartar (optional)
4 tablespoons icing sugar

To make the pastry, sift the flour and salt into a bowl. Rub in the fat until the mixture resembles fine breadcrumbs. Stir in sufficient water to make a fairly stiff dough. Knead lightly, then cover and chill for 30 minutes.

Roll out the dough and use to line a 23 cm (9 inch) flan tin. Line the flan case with greaseproof paper and dried beans. Bake blind in a preheated moderately hot oven, 190°C (375°F), Gas Mark 5, for 25 minutes or until golden brown and firm. Remove the beans and paper and allow to cool.

For the filling, put the sultanas and water in a saucepan and bring to the boil. Stir in the brown sugar and remove from the heat. Pour about 4 tablespoons of the mixture into a bowl and mix in the butter and flour. Return this to the saucepan and cook, stirring, until thickened. Remove from the heat and beat in the egg yolks and lemon rind and juice. Pour this filling into the pastry shell.

For the meringue, whisk the egg whites until frothy. Add the cream of tartar if using, and continue whisking until stiff. Gradually beat in the icing sugar.

Spoon the meringue over the filling, spreading it to the pastry rim. Bake in a preheated moderate oven, 180°C (350°F), Gas Mark 4, for 10 to 15 minutes or until the meringue is set and lightly golden brown.

Serves 6

Orange Salad

6 large juicy oranges
2 tablespoons gin
125 g (4 oz) sugar

Pare the rind from one orange and cut it into thin shreds. Peel the remaining oranges and remove the white pith from all six. Slice the oranges and put into a serving bowl. Sprinkle over the gin.

Put the sugar and shredded rind into a saucepan and heat gently, stirring until the sugar has melted. Continue heating until the syrup is golden brown and begins to bubble, then pour quickly over the oranges.

Leave for 30 minutes, then chill. Serve with single cream.

Serves 6

Champagne Sorbet

300 g (10 oz) sugar
250 ml (8 fl oz) water
600 ml (1 pint) sparkling white wine
3 tablespoons lemon juice
2 egg whites
4 tablespoons icing sugar

Dissolve the sugar in the water in a saucepan over low heat, then bring to the boil. Boil for about 5 minutes or until thick but not beginning to brown. Cool, then stir in 350 ml (12 fl oz) of the wine and the lemon juice. Pour into freezer trays and freeze for about 1 hour or until mushy.

Pour the mixture into a bowl and beat well for 2 minutes. Return to the freezer trays and freeze for a further 30 minutes. Beat again. Repeat the freezing and beating every 30 minutes for the next 2 hours.

Beat the egg whites until stiff. Gradually beat in the icing sugar.

Beat the frozen mixture well to break down the ice crystals, then fold in the meringue. Return to the freezer and freeze until firm.

About 30 minutes before required, put the sorbet in the refrigerator to soften slightly. Before serving, pour a little of wine over each portion.

Serves 8

Frozen Butterscotch Mousse

125 g (4 oz) brown sugar
25 g (1 oz) butter
pinch of salt
120 ml (4 fl oz) water
4 egg yolks
250 ml (8 fl oz) double cream
1 ½ teaspoons vanilla essence

Put the sugar, butter and salt in a saucepan. Stir until the sugar has dissolved and the butter melted, then bring to the boil. Boil for 1 minute. Stir in the water and cook until the butterscotch mixture is smooth and syrupy.

Beat the egg yolks in a heatproof bowl. Gradually beat in the butterscotch syrup. Place the bowl over a pan of simmering water and heat, beating, until the mixture is light and fluffy. Cool.

Whip the cream with the vanilla essence until thick. Fold into the butterscotch mixture. Pour into a decorative freezerproof mould and freeze until firm.

Transfer the mousse to the refrigerator 30 minutes before serving. To turn out, dip the mould quickly into hot water and invert onto a serving plate; the mousse should slide out. Serve with fresh soft fruit.

Serves 6

Chicken Stuffed Ham Rolls

500 g (1 lb) cooked chicken meat, diced
150 ml (1/4 pint) mayonnaise
8 tablespoons chopped parsley
8 tablespoons chopped celery leaves
12 black olives, stoned and finely chopped
1 large green pepper, cored, seeded and finely chopped
salt and pepper
16 slices of cooked ham
1 lettuce

Mix together the chicken, mayonnaise, parsley, celery leaves, olives, green pepper and salt and pepper to taste. Spread on the ham slices and roll up. Arrange on a serving platter lined with lettuce leaves.
Serves 16

Tuna Mousse

7 g (¼ oz) powdered gelatine
120 ml (4 fl oz) water
175 ml (6 fl oz) mayonnaise
1 tablespoon lemon juice
¼ teaspoon paprika
pinch of cayenne pepper
½ teaspoon salt
1 x 198 g (7 oz) can tuna fish, drained and flaked
2 celery sticks, finely chopped
2 tablespoons minced green pepper
150 ml (¼ pint) double cream
TO GARNISH:
lettuce leaves
watercress

Dissolve the gelatine in the water, then stir in the mayonnaise, lemon juice, paprika, cayenne and salt. When well mixed, fold in the tuna, celery and green pepper. Whip the cream until stiff and fold in. Pour into a 1 litre (2 pint) decorative mould and chill until set.

Turn out onto a serving plate and garnish with lettuce leaves and watercress.

Serves 6

Nutty Cheese Log

250 g (8 oz) cottage cheese
50 g (2 oz) Danish blue cheese, crumbled
6 black olives, stoned and chopped
2 tablespoons chopped pimento
2 tablespoons very finely chopped green pepper
1 tablespoon chopped parsley
40 g (1½ oz) butter
½ teaspoon paprika
125 g (4 oz) walnuts, finely chopped

Mix together the cottage cheese and Danish blue cheese, then beat in the olives, pimento, green pepper, parsley, butter and paprika. Shape into a log about 5 cm (2 inches) in diameter. Wrap in greaseproof paper and chill until firm.

Coat the log with the chopped nuts. Wrap in fresh greaseproof paper and chill until ready to serve. Serve cut into slices.

Makes 20 slices

Hot Crabmeat Canapés

25 g (1 oz) butter
½ small onion, finely chopped
½ small green pepper, cored, seeded and finely chopped
1 x 117 g (6 oz) can crabmeat, flaked
150 g (5 oz) mature Cheddar cheese, grated
4 tablespoons tomato ketchup
2 teaspoons Worcestershire sauce
pinch of cayenne pepper

Melt the butter in a saucepan. Add the onion and green pepper and fry until softened. Add the remaining ingredients and cook gently, stirring, until the cheese has melted and the mixture is hot. Spread onto savoury biscuits or small toast rounds or squares and serve hot.

Makes about 40 canapés

Tarragon Egg Puffs

2 streaky bacon rashers, derinded and finely diced
4 hard-boiled eggs, finely chopped
2 tablespoons double cream
1 teaspoon tarragon vinegar
1 teaspoon dried tarragon
40 small savoury biscuits (approximately)
mayonnaise

Fry the bacon in its own fat until it is crisp. Drain on kitchen paper.

Mix together the eggs, bacon, cream, vinegar and tarragon. Chill until firm.

Spread the mixture onto the savoury biscuits and top each with a thin layer of mayonnaise. Grill for about 1 minute or until the tops are lightly browned. Serve immediately.

Makes about 40 puffs

Olives on Horseback

30 large pimento-stuffed green olives
250 g (8 oz) mature Cheddar cheese, grated
10 streaky bacon rashers, derinded

Halve the olives lengthways and scoop out the pimento. Finely chop the pimento and mix thoroughly into the cheese. Stuff the olive halves with the cheese mixture and press the halves back together.

Stretch the bacon rashers with the back of a knife, then cut each rasher into 3 pieces. Wrap each stuffed olive in a piece of bacon and secure with a wooden cocktail stick.

Grill the olives for 4 to 5 minutes on each side or until the bacon is crisp.

Makes 30 olives

Japanese Almonds

625 g (1¼ lb) blanched almonds
50 g (2 oz) butter
2 tablespoons soy sauce
2 tablespoons dry sherry
½ teaspoon ground ginger
garlic salt

Spread the almonds in a shallow baking tin and toast in a preheated cool oven, 150°C (300°F), Gas Mark 2, for 20 minutes.

Meanwhile, melt the butter in a saucepan. Stir in the soy sauce, sherry and ginger. Pour over the almonds and continue toasting, stirring occasionally, for 15 to 20 minutes. Sprinkle with garlic salt to taste, then spread out on kitchen paper and leave to dry and cool.

Serves 12 to 16

Seeded Biscuits

24 water biscuits
50 g (2 oz) butter, melted
caraway, poppy or sesame seeds

Brush one side of each biscuit with melted butter. Sprinkle with caraway, poppy or sesame seeds and arrange the biscuits on baking sheets. Heat in a preheated moderate oven, 180°C (350°F), Gas Mark 4, for 5 minutes or until crisp and hot.

Makes 24 biscuits

Liptoi

250 g (8 oz) curd cheese
250 g (8 oz) butter
½ teaspoon paprika
½ teaspoon caraway seeds
½ small onion, grated

Beat the ingredients together, adding more paprika, and caraway seeds to taste. Serve with small savoury biscuits.
Serves 10 to 12

Apple and Date Dip

250 g (8 oz) cream cheese
2 red-skinned apples, cored and grated
12 dates, stoned and finely chopped
milk
apple and date slices to garnish

Beat together the cream cheese, apples and dates and add enough milk to give a dipping consistency. Cover and chill for at least 2 hours before serving. Serve garnished with apple and date slices.
Serves 6 to 8

Spicy Tuna Dip

1 x 198 g (7 oz) can tuna fish, drained and flaked
125 g (4 oz) cream cheese
1 tablespoon mayonnaise
1 tablespoon chopped capers
½ teaspoon soy sauce
1 teaspoon horseradish sauce
¼ teaspoon garlic salt
¼ teaspoon celery salt
milk (as necessary)
chicory leaves and capers to garnish

Mix together all the ingredients. If the mixture is too thick for dipping, add a little milk. Serve on a bed of chicory, garnished with capers.
Serves 6 to 8

Dill Cheese Dip

125 g (4 oz) cottage cheese
125 g (4 oz) cream cheese
½ onion, grated
6 pimento-stuffed green olives, chopped
½ teaspoon dried dill
salt
single cream
chopped dill or chives to garnish

Beat together the cheeses, onion, olives, dill and salt to taste. Add enough cream to give the mixture a dipping consistency. Serve garnished with dill or chives.
Serves 6

Gammon with Spicy Sauce

1 x 2.75 kg (6 lb) boned piece of gammon, soaked then parboiled for 1 hour
250 ml (8 fl oz) orange juice
150 g (5 oz) brown sugar
2 teaspoons dry mustard
¼ teaspoon ground cloves
pinch of grated nutmeg
½ teaspoon ground ginger
3 teaspoons rum essence
whole cloves
75 g (3 oz) raisins
1 tablespoon lemon juice
1 tablespoon cornflour
1 tablespoon water
watercress to garnish

Remove the skin from the gammon and most of the fat, leaving a layer about 3 mm (⅛ inch) thick. Place in a bowl and pierce all over with a fork.

Put the orange juice, sugar, mustard, spices and 2 teaspoons of the rum essence in a saucepan and bring to the boil, stirring. Pour over the gammon and leave for 4 hours.

Transfer the gammon to a roasting pan and bake in a preheated moderate oven, 160°C (325°F), Gas Mark 3, for 1 hour.

Score the gammon and stud with the cloves. Increase the oven temperature to hot, 220°C (425°F), Gas Mark 7, and bake for a further 30 minutes, basting frequently.

Transfer the gammon to a warmed serving dish and keep hot. Add the raisins and lemon juice to the pan juices and mix well. Dissolve the cornflour in the water and stir in. Cook, stirring, on top of the stove until the mixture thickens. Stir in the remaining rum essence.

Garnish the gammon with watercress, carve and serve with the sauce.

Serves 10 to 12

Apple and Courgette Salad

150 ml (1/4 pint) oil
4 tablespoons wine vinegar
2 tablespoons lemon juice
2 teaspoons caster sugar
2 teaspoons dried basil
salt and pepper
6 Golden Delicious apples, cored and chopped
1 kg (2 lb) courgettes, thinly sliced
1 Spanish onion, thinly sliced
2 green peppers, cored, seeded and thinly sliced

Mix together the oil, vinegar, lemon juice, sugar, basil and salt and pepper to taste in a large bowl. Add the apples and toss well to coat. Add the courgettes, onion and green peppers and fold the ingredients together thoroughly. Cover and chill.

Toss again just before serving.

Serves 12

Chilli con Carne

3 tablespoons beef dripping
3 onions, finely chopped
2 cloves garlic, crushed
2 medium green peppers, cored, seeded and diced
2 red chillis, seeded and diced (optional)
1.5 kg (3 lb) lean minced beef
3 x 397 g (14 oz) cans tomatoes
1 x 65 g (2¼ oz) can tomato purée
2 teaspoons chilli powder (or more to taste)
2 bay leaves
salt and pepper
3 x 425 g (15 oz) cans red kidney beans, drained

Heat the dripping in a large saucepan. Add the onions, garlic, green peppers and chillis, if used, and fry until softened. Add the beef and continue frying, stirring frequently, until browned. Stir in the tomatoes with their juice, tomato purée, chilli powder, bay leaves and salt and pepper to taste. Cover and simmer for 1 hour.

Stir in the kidney beans and simmer, uncovered, for 30 minutes. Discard the bay leaves before serving.

Serves 10 to 12

Swedish Meatballs

1.5 kg (3 lb) lean minced beef
125 g (4 oz) Parmesan cheese, grated
2 onions, finely chopped
1 clove garlic, crushed
3 large eggs, beaten
1 teaspoon grated nutmeg
1 teaspoon paprika
salt and pepper
75 g (3 oz) butter
SAUCE:
600 ml (1 pint) beef stock
2 teaspoons tomato purée
2 egg yolks, beaten
450 ml (¾ pint) fresh sour cream
4 tablespoons dried dill

Mix together the beef, cheese, onions, garlic, eggs, nutmeg, paprika, salt and pepper. Form the mixture into walnut-sized balls.

Melt half the butter in a frying pan. Add the meatballs, in batches, and brown on all sides. Use more butter as needed and transfer the meatballs to a baking dish as they brown.

Put the stock and tomato purée in a basin over a pan of simmering water. Mix together, then add the egg yolks. Cook, stirring, for 5 minutes. Do not let the bowl get too hot or the egg yolks will scramble. Remove from the heat and stir in the sour cream and dill. Pour this sauce over the meatballs.

Cook in a preheated cool oven, 150°C (300°F), Gas Mark 2, for 20 minutes. Serve hot in a flameproof serving dish placed over a spirit burner.

Serves 10 to 12

Devilled Eggs

12 hard-boiled eggs, finely chopped
2 teaspoons minced onion
4 streaky bacon rashers, derinded, fried until crisp and crumbled
½ teaspoon dry mustard
120 ml (4 fl oz) mayonnaise
dash of Tabasco sauce
salt and pepper
125 g (4 oz) Cheddar cheese, grated
watercress to garnish

Mix together the eggs, onion, bacon, mustard, mayonnaise, Tabasco and salt and pepper to taste. Divide the mixture into 14 portions and shape each into an 'egg'. Coat with the grated cheese.

Chill the devilled eggs before serving, on a platter garnished with watercress.

Makes 14

Jellied Pressed Beef

1 x 2.25 kg (5 lb) brisket of beef
1 calf's foot
2 onions
6 whole cloves
1 celery stick with leaves, halved
2 cloves garlic
1 bay leaf
1½ tablespoons salt
6 black peppercorns
1 tablespoon Worcestershire sauce
1 egg white
1 egg shell, crushed
TO GARNISH:
parsley sprigs
tomato wedges
cucumber slices

Chop the brisket (with bones) into rectangular pieces about 7.5 x 2.5 cm (3 x 1 inch). Place in a large saucepan with the calf's foot, onions stuck with the cloves, celery, garlic, bay leaf, salt, peppercorns and Worcestershire sauce. Add sufficient water to cover and bring to the boil. Skim, then simmer for about 3½ hours or until the beef is tender.

Remove the pieces of beef from the pan and cool slightly. Boil the liquid rapidly until it is reduced by about two thirds. Skim off any fat, then strain the liquid through a clean tea towel into a clean pan.

Beat the egg white slightly, then add to the pan with the egg shell. Bring the liquid back to the boil, beating the egg white and shell into the liquid. When the liquid rises in the pan, remove from the heat and leave to settle. Strain it again through a clean damp tea towel or muslin.

Remove the bones from the beef and pack the meat into a mould. Pour over the clarified liquid and cover with a plate and then a weight. Chill overnight.

Unmould and serve garnished with parsley, tomato and cucumber.
Serves 8 to 10

Spicy Tomato Aspic

4 x 397 g (14 oz) cans tomatoes
2 teaspoons black peppercorns
2 teaspoons sugar
1 teaspoon celery salt
2 large onions, sliced
6 whole cloves
25 g (1 oz) powdered gelatine
250 ml (8 fl oz) water
3 tablespoons lemon juice
1 tablespoon Worcestershire sauce
1 teaspoon horseradish sauce
salt
chicory to serve

Put the tomatoes with their juice, peppercorns, sugar, celery salt, onions and cloves in a saucepan and simmer for 30 minutes. Strain the mixture, rubbing tomatoes through the sieve. Soften the gelatine in the water, then add to the tomato mixture and stir until dissolved. Stir in the lemon juice, Worcestershire and horseradish sauces, and salt to taste. Pour into a 1.5 litre (2½ pint) ring mould and chill for 20 minutes.

Stir the tomato mixture, then leave to chill for a further 20 minutes. Stir again and leave until set.

Turn out onto a serving dish lined with endive leaves and fill the centre with endive. Serve with Creamy blue cheese dressing.

Serves 8

Mandarin Chicken

24 chicken breasts, skinned
175 g (6 oz) butter, melted
4 x 212 g (7½ oz) cans mandarin oranges
1.2 litres (2 pints) chicken stock (approximately)
4 tablespoons cornflour
2 teaspoons mild curry powder
2 tablespoons lemon juice
salt and pepper
1 large onion, very finely chopped
3 large green peppers, cored, seeded and thinly sliced
500 g (1 lb) dried dates, halved and stoned

Brush the chicken breasts all over with melted butter and arrange in two roasting pans in one layer. Pour over the rest of the butter. Bake in a preheated moderate oven, 180°C (350°F), Gas Mark 4, for 1 hour or until cooked through.

Meanwhile, drain the mandarin oranges, reserving 600 ml (1 pint) of the juice. (If there isn't enough, add a little more stock.) Dissolve the cornflour in a little of the stock and put in a saucepan with the remaining stock and the reserved juice. Stir in the curry powder, lemon juice, salt and pepper and bring to the boil. Simmer, stirring, until thickened and clear.

Add the onion and green peppers and simmer for 5 minutes or until just tender. Stir in the mandarin oranges and dates.

Pour the sauce over the chicken breasts and keep warm in the oven until serving time.

Serves 24

Creamy Blue Cheese Dressing

125 g (4 oz) blue cheese
3 tablespoons single cream
120 ml (4 fl oz) mayonnaise
1 teaspoon made mustard
6 tablespoons oil
4 tablespoons wine vinegar
salt and pepper

Mash the cheese with the cream until well blended. Beat in the remaining ingredients with salt and pepper to taste. Store in a covered container in the refrigerator.

Makes about 350 ml (12 fl oz) dressing

Tongue Salad Platter

150 ml (¼ pint) vinaigrette dressing
150 ml (¼ pint) mayonnaise
salt and pepper
1.5 kg (3 lb) cottage cheese
750 g (1½ lb) potatoes, cooked and diced
8 hard-boiled eggs, chopped
1 large green pepper, cored, seeded and diced
3 canned pimentos, diced
1 small onion, minced
6 tablespoons chopped parsley
TO SERVE:
lettuce and chicory leaves
radishes
black olives
16 slices of cooked tongue

Mix together the vinaigrette dressing, mayonnaise and salt and pepper to taste. Beat in the cottage cheese, then fold in the potatoes, eggs, green pepper, pimentos, onion and parsley. Spoon the mixture into a lightly oiled 3 litre (5 pint) ring mould. Chill for at least 2 hours.

Line a serving dish with lettuce and chicory leaves. Loosen the cheese salad mould and turn out onto the dish. Fill the centre with radishes and olives and surround with the rolled tongue slices.

Serves 16

Macaroni Fish Salad

500 g (1 lb) cut macaroni
salt and pepper
300 ml (½ pint) mayonnaise
300 ml (½ pint) milk
250 ml (8 fl oz) vinaigrette dressing
1 kg (2 lb) white fish fillets, cooked, skinned and flaked
250 g (8 oz) frozen shelled prawns, thawed
6 celery sticks, thinly sliced
8 spring onions, chopped
500 g (1 lb) white cabbage, cored and shredded
TO GARNISH:
4 hard-boiled eggs, sliced
watercress

Cook the macaroni in boiling salted water until tender. Drain and cool. Mix together the mayonnaise, milk, vinaigrette dressing and salt and pepper to taste, then fold in the macaroni. Add the fish, prawns, celery, spring onions and cabbage and fold together thoroughly. Pile into a serving dish and chill.

Serve garnished with egg slices and watercress.

Serves 16

Baked Orange Cheesecake

250 g (8 oz) rich tea biscuits, crushed
250 g (8 oz) butter, melted
3 x 250 g (8 oz) packets cream cheese
250 g (8 oz) caster sugar
3 eggs, beaten
½ teaspoon orange-flower water
1 x 212 g (7½ oz) can mandarin oranges, drained

Mix together the crushed biscuits and 100 g (4 oz) of the butter. Use to line the bottom and sides of a 25 cm (10 inch) flan tin with a removable base. Chill while preparing the filling.

Beat together the cream cheese, sugar, eggs, orange-flower water and remaining melted butter. Pour into the crumb crust. Bake in the centre of a preheated hot oven, 230°C (450°F), Gas Mark 8, for 15 minutes. Cool completely.

Just before serving, decorate with the mandarin orange segments.

Serves 12

Cherry Bavarois

5 eggs
125 g (4 oz) caster sugar
15 g (½ oz) powdered gelatine
150 ml (¼ pint) water
2 tablespoons Kirsch
450 ml (¾ pint) double cream
150 g (5 oz) glacé cherries, chopped
32 sponge fingers (approximately)
whipped cream and halved glacé cherries to decorate

Put the eggs and sugar in a heatproof bowl placed over a pan of simmering water. Whisk until the mixture is pale and very thick. (If using an electric beater, no heat is necessary.) Remove the bowl from the heat.

Dissolve the gelatine in 4 tablespoons of the water and stir into the egg mixture with 1 tablespoon of the Kirsch. Chill until mixture is the consistency of unbeaten egg white.

Whip the cream until stiff and fold into the egg mixture, then fold in the chopped cherries. Chill for 15 minutes while preparing the mould.

Line the sides and bottom of a 1 litre (2 pint) plain slant-sided mould with dampened greaseproof paper. Mix together the remaining Kirsch and water in a shallow dish. Dip the sugar side of the sponge fingers into the liquid just to moisten them and use to line the sides of the mould, sugared side against the mould. Pour the cherry mixture carefully into the mould. Cover and chill overnight.

Turn out the bavarois onto a serving plate and decorate with whirls of cream and glacé cherries.
Serves 10 to 12

Cheese Surprise Burgers

1 kg (2 lb) lean minced beef
1 egg, beaten
salt and pepper
¾ teaspoon dried thyme
125 g (4 oz) cream cheese

Mix together the beef, egg, salt and pepper to taste and thyme, using your hands to combine the ingredients thoroughly. Divide into 12 portions and shape each into a flat cake about 10 cm (4 inches) in diameter.

Cut the cheese into six portions and shape each into a round about 5 cm (2 inches) in diameter. Place a cheese round on six of the beef cakes and cover with the remaining beef cakes. Press the edges together to seal.

Grill the burgers for about 8 minutes on each side or until cooked to your liking. Serve in soft rolls or baps with tomato ketchup, mustard and pickles.

Serves 6

Porcupine Meatballs

1 kg (2 lb) lean minced beef
75 g (3 oz) long-grain rice
2 eggs, beaten
salt and pepper
2 x 298 g (10½ oz) cans condensed tomato soup
250 ml (8 fl oz) water
2 teaspoons Worcestershire sauce

Mix together the beef, rice, eggs, salt and pepper to taste and 8 tablespoons of the undiluted soup. Shape into walnut-sized balls and place in a casserole.

Put the remaining soup, the water and Worcestershire sauce in a saucepan and bring to the boil, stirring. Pour over the meatballs. Cover the dish tightly and cook in a preheated moderate oven, 180°C (350°F), Gas Mark 4, for 45 minutes or until the meatballs are cooked through.

Serves 8 to 10

Cheese surprise Burgers; Sausages in jackets (page 70); Porcupine meatballs.

Sausages in Jackets

6 large pork sausages
6 slices of white bread, crusts removed
made mustard
sweet pickle
50 g (2 oz) butter, melted

Fry or grill the sausages until they are cooked. Drain well on kitchen paper. Spread each slice of bread with mustard and then with pickle. Place a sausage across one corner of each slice of bread and roll up. Secure with wooden cocktail sticks.

Brush the bread with melted butter and grill until the bread jackets are toasted and golden brown all over.

Serves 6

Illustrated on page 69.

Pineapple Bacon Toasts

3 eggs
350 ml (12 fl oz) pineapple juice
½ teaspoon salt
6 slices of stale white bread, 1 cm (½ inch) thick, cut into fingers
6 streaky bacon rashers, derinded
50 g (2 oz) butter
6 canned pineapple rings
parsley sprigs to garnish

Beat together the eggs, pineapple juice and salt in a shallow dish. Add the bread fingers and turn to coat well with the egg mixture. Leave to soak while frying the bacon in a dry frying pan until crisp. Remove the bacon from the pan and keep hot.

Melt the butter in the pan. Add the soaked bread fingers, in batches, and fry until golden brown all over, using more butter as necessary. Arrange them on a warmed serving dish and keep hot.

Put the pineapple rings in the pan and fry until lightly golden. Arrange the pineapple and bacon on the bread fingers and garnish with parsley.

Serves 6

Pork and Bean Bake

2 x 446 g ($15\frac{3}{4}$ oz) cans baked beans
125 g (4 oz) brown sugar
6 pork sparerib chops
salt and pepper
French mustard
6 tablespoons tomato ketchup

Mix together the baked beans and half the sugar and pour into a wide shallow baking dish. Arrange the chops on the beans, in one layer, pressing them down slightly. Sprinkle each chop with salt and pepper, then spread lightly with mustard. Scatter over the rest of the brown sugar and top each chop with a tablespoon of ketchup.

Bake in a preheated moderate oven, 160°C (325°F), Gas Mark 3, for $1\frac{1}{2}$ hours or until the chops are cooked through.

Serves 6

Triple Decker Sandwiches

1 unsliced white sandwich loaf, crusts removed
butter
4 hard-boiled eggs, chopped
5 tablespoons mayonnaise
½ teaspoon made mustard
3 tablespoons mustard and cress
125 g (4 oz) Cheddar cheese, grated
4 tablespoons sweet pickle
175 g (6 oz) cottage cheese
3 tomatoes, diced
parsley sprigs and tomato wedges to garnish

Cut the loaf of bread into slices and spread with butter.

Mix together the eggs, mayonnaise, mustard and mustard and cress.

Combine the Cheddar cheese and pickle in a separate bowl.

Mix together the cottage cheese and tomatoes in a third bowl.

Sandwich the bread slices together with alternate layers of the different fillings to make triple decker sandwiches. Cut the sandwiches diagonally into quarters and arrange on a serving plate. Chill until required.

Serve, garnished with parsley sprigs and tomato wedges.

Serves 10 to 12

Citrus Jelly Whip

600 ml (1 pint) packet lemon jelly
200 ml (⅓ pint) boiling water
7 g (¼ oz) powdered gelatine
2 tablespoons water
300 ml (½ pint) orange juice
juice of ½ lemon
1 x 426 ml (15 fl oz) can evaporated milk
1 teaspoon grated orange rind
whipped cream and crystallized lemon and orange slices to decorate

Dissolve the jelly in the boiling water. Dissolve the gelatine in the water. Mix the two together and add the orange and lemon juices. Chill until almost on the point of setting.

Whip the evaporated milk with the orange rind until it is very thick and mousse-like. Beat in the jelly mixture. Spoon into 6 serving dishes and chill until set. Serve decorated with whirls of whipped cream and crystallized fruit slices.

Serves 6

Peanut Crispy Bars

75 g (3 oz) Rice Krispies
225 g (7 oz) salted peanuts
125 g (4 oz) sugar
175 g (6 oz) golden syrup
4 tablespoons peanut butter
½ teaspoon vanilla essence

Mix together the cereal and peanuts. Put the sugar and syrup in a saucepan and bring to the boil, stirring to dissolve the sugar. Remove from the heat and stir in the peanut butter and vanilla. Fold in the cereal mixture.

Pour into a greased 20 cm (8 inch) square baking tin and press into the corners. Cool, then cut into bars.

Makes 32 bars

Chocolate Chip and Nut Cookies

125 g (4 oz) plain flour
½ teaspoon bicarbonate of soda
½ teaspoon salt
100 g (4 oz) butter, softened
75 g (3 oz) granulated sugar
50 g (2 oz) brown sugar
½ teaspoon vanilla essence
1 egg, beaten
175 g (6 oz) chocolate dots
50 g (2 oz) walnuts, chopped

Sift together the flour, bicarbonate of soda and salt. Cream the butter and sugars together until fluffy, then fold in the flour mixture. Add the vanilla and egg and beat until well mixed. If the mixture seems dry, add a little water. Fold in the chocolate dots and nuts.

Drop well rounded small spoonsful of the mixture onto greased baking sheets, spacing them to allow for spreading. Bake in a preheated moderately hot oven, 190°C (375°F), Gas Mark 5, for 10 to 12 minutes or until golden brown. Cool on a wire rack.

Makes about 50 cookies

Caramel Dream Cakes

1 x 69 g (2½ oz) packet butterscotch dessert mix
2 large bananas, sliced
250 g (8 oz) vanilla caramels
150 ml (¼ pint) evaporated milk
6 individual trifle sponge cakes

Make the dessert according to the directions on the packet. Fold in the bananas and chill.

Meanwhile, put the caramels and milk in a saucepan and heat gently, stirring, until the caramels have melted.

Put the sponge cakes on six individual plates and top with the banana mixture. Pour over the caramel sauce and serve.

Serves 6

UFO Party Cake

300 g (10 oz) butter
300 g (10 oz) caster sugar
5 large eggs
300 g (10 oz) self-raising flour
¼ teaspoon salt
4-5 tablespoons milk
jam
500 g (1 lb) icing sugar
about 6 tablespoons warm water
coloured jelly sweets
silver balls
chocolate sticks

Cream together the butter and caster sugar until soft and fluffy. Beat in the eggs gradually. Sift in the flour and salt and fold in. Add just enough milk to give the batter a dropping consistency.

Divide the batter between two greased and lined round sandwich tins, one 20 cm (8 inches) in diameter, the other 15 cm (6 inches). Bake the two cakes in a preheated moderate oven, 180°C (350°F), Gas Mark 4, for about 40 to 45 minutes or until the cakes spring back when lightly pressed in the centres. Turn out and cool on a wire rack.

Cut each cake in half through the centre to make two semi-circles. Sandwich together the halves of each cake with jam. Spread jam on the cut edges of the smaller cake and press against the cut edges of the larger cake. Place on a board or tray lined with foil.

Sift the icing sugar into a bowl and mix in enough warm water to make a thick icing. Use this to cover the assembled cake completely. Place the coloured sweets on the top of the smaller cake to resemble lights, and spell out your child's name in silver balls on the larger cake. Make the legs and antenna with chocolate sticks.

Serves 12

Ice lollies

175 ml (6 fl oz) orange juice
2 x 150 g (5 oz) cartons fruit yogurt
½ teaspoon vanilla essence

Mix together the ingredients and pour into ice cube trays with dividers or into small paper cups. Freeze until mushy, then insert a small wooden stick into each. Return to the freezer and freeze until hard.

Makes 14

JOHN

Chilled Piquant Chicken

3 tablespoons oil
4 or 8 chicken pieces
300 ml (½ pint) chicken stock
150 ml (¼ pint) dry white wine
150 ml (¼ pint) red wine vinegar
juice of 1 lemon
2 cloves garlic, crushed
1 teaspoon grated orange rind
2-3 bay leaves
salt and pepper

Heat the oil in a deep frying pan. Add the chicken pieces and brown on all sides. Mix together the remaining ingredients, with salt and pepper to taste, and pour over the chicken pieces. Bring to the boil, then cover and simmer for 1 hour or until the chicken pieces are tender.

Remove from the heat and allow to cool. Pour the chicken and liquid into a polythene container, cover and chill well. Take to the picnic in the container and use paper napkins to serve.

Serves 4

Courgette Quiche

SHORTCRUST PASTRY:
250 g (8 oz) plain flour
pinch of salt
50 g (2 oz) butter
50 g (2 oz) lard
water to mix
FILLING:
40 g (1½ oz) butter
750 g (1½ lb) courgettes, sliced
75 g (3 oz) Gruyère cheese, grated
3 eggs
150 ml (¼ pint) single cream
salt and pepper

Make the shortcrust pastry as for Sultana Meringue Pie (page 44). Roll out the dough and use to line a 23 cm (9 inch) quiche dish.

Melt the butter in a frying pan. Add the courgettes and fry until almost tender. Drain on kitchen paper and arrange in the pastry case, cut sides up. Sprinkle with the cheese.

Beat together the eggs, cream and salt and pepper to taste and pour into the pastry case. Bake in a preheated moderately hot oven, 200°C (400°F), Gas Mark 6, for 35 minutes or until the pastry is golden and the filling is set. Allow to cool, then cover with foil. Take to the picnic in the dish.

Serves 6 to 8

Bean Salad

4 tablespoons treacle
2 tablespoons oil
2 tablespoons cider vinegar
1 tablespoon made mustard
3 tablespoons sweet pickle
2 x 446 g (15¾ oz) cans baked beans
3 celery sticks, thinly sliced
2 carrots, diced
3 spring onions, finely chopped
50 g (2 oz) mature Cheddar cheese, diced
2 tomatoes, chopped
salt and pepper

Mix together the treacle, oil, vinegar, mustard and pickle in a bowl. Add the remaining ingredients with salt and pepper to taste and mix well. Pour into a polythene container, cover and chill, preferably overnight. Take to the picnic in the container.

Serves 6 to 8

NOTE: This salad is delicious with hard-boiled eggs.

French Ham and Egg Sandwiches

2 French loaves
125 g (4 oz) butter
6 spring onions, finely chopped
1 green pepper, cored, seeded and diced
250 g (8 oz) cooked ham, diced
6 tablespoons mayonnaise
1 tablespoon French mustard
6 eggs, beaten
120 ml (4 fl oz) milk
pinch of garlic powder
salt and pepper

Cut the ends off the loaves, then cut each in half to make four 15 cm (6 inch) lengths, approximately. Split them open, without cutting all the way through, and butter the cut surfaces, using half the butter.

Mix together the spring onions, green pepper, ham, mayonnaise and mustard. Divide between the bread lengths, spreading the mixture on the bottom halves.

Beat together the eggs, milk, and garlic powder with salt and pepper to taste. Melt the remaining butter in a saucepan and add the egg mixture. Cook gently, stirring, until scrambled. Spread over the ham mixture and press the sandwiches together to enclose the filling. Cool, then wrap in foil to take to the picnic.

Makes 4

Orange Nut Shortbread

200 g (7 oz) plain flour
pinch of salt
50 g (2 oz) sugar
2½ teaspoons grated orange rind
125 g (4 oz) butter
125 g (4 oz) walnuts, finely chopped
3 tablespoons orange juice
50 g (2 oz) icing sugar

Mix together the flour, salt, sugar and 2 teaspoons of the orange rind. Rub in the butter until the mixture resembles breadcrumbs. Mix in three-quarters of the walnuts and 1 tablespoon of the orange juice.

Form the dough into a ball, adding more orange juice if it is too dry, and place in a greased 18 x 28 cm (7 x 11 inch) Swiss roll tin. Press out firmly to make an even layer in the tin. Bake in a preheated moderate oven, 160°C (325°F), Gas Mark 3, for 40 to 45 minutes or until golden brown.

Cool slightly, then sprinkle with the remaining walnuts. Mix together the icing sugar and remaining orange rind and juice and drizzle this evenly over the shortbread. Cut into bars, then leave to cool completely in the tin. Wrap in foil to take to the picnic.
Makes about 30

Stuffed Rump Steaks

3 x 500 g (1 lb) rump steaks, 2.5 cm (1 inch) thick
120 ml (4 fl oz) red wine
4 tablespoons oil
4 tablespoons soy sauce
½ teaspoon grated nutmeg
75 g (3 oz) butter
2 medium green peppers, cored, seeded and very finely chopped
2 onions, minced
3 celery sticks, very finely chopped
250 g (8 oz) fresh breadcrumbs
2 tablespoons sweet pickle
salt and pepper

Cut off any fat from the steaks then cut a deep pocket in each steak, being careful not to cut through to the outside. Place the steaks in a shallow dish, in one layer.

Mix together the wine, oil, soy sauce and nutmeg and sprinkle over the steaks. Leave to marinate for at least 1 hour, turning occasionally.

Melt the butter in a frying pan. Add the green peppers, onions and celery and fry until softened. Remove from the heat and stir in the breadcrumbs, pickle and salt and pepper to taste.

Drain the steaks, reserving the marinade. Carefully spoon the stuffing into the steak pockets and sew the opening with a trussing needle and strong thread.

Place the steaks on the barbecue grid, about 10 cm (4 inches) from the coals. Cook for 10 to 15 minutes on each side, according to taste, basting frequently with the reserved marinade. Cut the steaks in half to serve.

Serves 6

Marinated Redcurrant Chicken

75 g (3 oz) redcurrant jelly
4 tablespoons lemon juice
4 tablespoons oil
4 tablespoons chicken stock
½ teaspoon dry mustard
½ teaspoon Worcestershire sauce
salt and pepper
4 or 8 chicken pieces

Melt the jelly in a saucepan. Stir in the lemon juice, oil, stock, mustard, Worcestershire sauce and salt and pepper to taste.

Arrange the chicken pieces in a shallow dish, in one layer, and pour over the jelly mixture. Cover and leave to marinate overnight.

Drain the chicken pieces, reserving the marinade, and place on the barbecue grid, about 15 cm (6 inches) above the coals. Cook for about 50 minutes or until the chicken is cooked through, turning frequently and basting with the reserved marinade.

Serves 4

Pear and Grape Coleslaw

500 g (1 lb) white cabbage, cored and shredded
6 spring onions, thinly sliced
3 celery sticks, thinly sliced
250 g (8 oz) seedless green grapes
150 ml (¼ pint) mayonnaise
150 ml (¼ pint) fresh sour cream
1 teaspoon grated orange rind
3 Conference pears, peeled, cored and sliced
2 tablespoons orange juice
salt and pepper
25 g (1 oz) flaked almonds, toasted

Mix together the cabbage, spring onions, celery and grapes in a bowl. Cover and chill. Mix together the mayonnaise, sour cream and orange rind; chill.

Just before serving, mix together the cabbage mixture and mayonnaise dressing. Sprinkle the pear slices with the orange juice to coat all over and add to the salad with salt and pepper to taste. Toss together thoroughly. Garnish with the toasted almonds.

Serves 6 to 8

Barbecued Potatoes

6 large potatoes
oil for brushing
salt

Brush the potato skins with oil and sprinkle with salt. Wrap the potatoes individually in a double thickness of foil. Put directly on the hot coals in the barbecue, or on the grid, and cook for 1 hour or until tender, turning once or twice during the cooking.

Serves 6

Barbecued Leg of Lamb

1 x 2.25 kg (5 lb) leg of lamb
2 cloves garlic, crushed
150 ml (¼ pint) red wine
5 tablespoons olive oil
5 tablespoons red wine vinegar
4 tablespoons chopped parsley
1 teaspoon mixed dried herbs
salt and pepper
small bunch of parsley

Bone the leg of lamb, without cutting all the way through, so that the meat can be opened flat.

Mix together the garlic, wine, oil, vinegar, chopped parsley, herbs and salt and pepper to taste. Lay the lamb on the barbecue grid, fat side up, about 15 cm (6 inches) above the coals. Baste with the wine mixture, using the bunch of parsley as the basting brush, and cook for 50 to 60 minutes or until the lamb is cooked through, turning occasionally and basting frequently.

Serves 6

Nutty Apple Pies

1 kg (2 lb) cooking apples, peeled, cored and thinly sliced
50 g (2 oz) brown sugar
¾ teaspoon ground cinnamon
¼ teaspoon grated nutmeg
125 g (4 oz) walnuts, finely chopped
SWEETCRUST PASTRY:
175 g (6 oz) plain flour
50 g (2 oz) granulated sugar
½ teaspoon salt
125 g (4 oz) butter
1 egg yolk

Mix together the apples, brown sugar, spices and half the walnuts. Divide between 6 individual baking dishes, about 10 cm (4 inches) in diameter and about 4 cm (1¾ inches) deep.

To make the pastry, mix together the flour, granulated sugar and salt and rub in the butter until the mixture resembles breadcrumbs. Stir in the egg yolk and the remaining nuts. If necessary, add a little water to bind the dough together.

Divide the dough into 6 portions and pat each one into a round about 15 cm (6 inches) in diameter. Place the dough rounds on the baking dishes and pinch over the edges to seal. Make a few slits in the top of each one.

Bake in a preheated moderate oven, 180°C (350°F), Gas Mark 4, for 40 to 45 minutes or until the crust is golden. Serve warm or cold.

Makes 6

Spicy Fruit Kebabs

2 oranges
2 red-skinned apples
2 bananas
16 pineapple chunks, fresh or canned
125 g (4 oz) butter
2 tablespoons sugar
1 teaspoon ground allspice or coriander

Cut each orange into 4 thick slices and halve each slice. Core the apples and cut each into 4 wedges. Cut each banana into 4 thick slices. Thread 2 orange pieces, 1 apple wedge, 1 banana slice and 2 pineapple chunks onto each of 8 skewers.

Melt the butter in a saucepan on the side of the barbecue. Stir in the sugar and spice.

Place the fruit kebabs on the barbecue grid, about 15 cm (6 inches) above the heat. Brush with the spice butter and cook for about 5 minutes, basting frequently and turning to brown on all sides.

Serves 8

Simnel Cake

500 g (1 lb) mixed dried fruit (sultanas, raisins, currants)
125 g (4 oz) glacé cherries, chopped
50 g (2 oz) chopped mixed candied peel
2 tablespoons rum
2 tablespoons orange juice
175 g (6 oz) butter
175 g (6 oz) caster sugar
3 eggs
200 g (7 oz) plain flour
1 teaspoon baking powder
1 teaspoon ground allspice
1 kg (2 lb) almond paste
2 tablespoons apricot jam, sieved
1 egg yolk
1 teaspoon water

Put the fruit, glacé cherries, peel, rum and orange juice in a bowl and mix well. Leave to soak for about 15 minutes.

Cream the butter and sugar together in another bowl until the mixture is pale and fluffy. Beat in the eggs, one at a time. Sift in the flour, baking powder and spice and fold in. Add the fruit mixture and combine thoroughly. Spoon half the mixture into a greased and lined deep round 18 cm (7 inch) cake tin and smooth the top.

Break off about one third of the almond paste and roll out to an 18 cm (7 inch) round. Place in the tin and cover with the rest of the cake mixture. Bake in a preheated moderate oven, 160°C (325°F), Gas Mark 3, for about 3 hours or until a skewer inserted into the centre of the cake comes out clean, and the cake has begun to shrink from the tin.

Roll out half the remaining almond paste to an 18 cm (7 inch) round. Brush the top of the cake with half the apricot jam and put on the round of almond paste. Form the rest of the almond paste into 11 balls. Put them around the edge of the cake, securing each one with a little apricot jam. Mix together the egg yolk and water and brush over the balls.

Return the cake to the oven and bake for a further 10 minutes or until the almond balls are golden brown. Leave in the tin to cool, then turn out. Tie a yellow ribbon around the cake before serving.

Makes an 18 cm (7 inch) cake

Roast Leg of Lamb with Herb Sauce

1 x 3 kg (6 lb) leg of lamb
2 small onions
4 whole cloves
2 cloves garlic
2 carrots, sliced
12 black peppercorns
12 juniper berries (optional)
4 parsley sprigs
2 bay leaves
2 mint sprigs
2 thyme sprigs
1 bottle dry white wine
3 tablespoons oil
salt and pepper
40 g (1½ oz) butter
3 shallots, finely chopped
25 g (1 oz) plain flour
1 x 411 g (14½ oz) can beef consommé
4 tablespoons chopped parsley
mint and parsley sprigs to garnish

Put the lamb in a polythene bag. Add the onions stuck with the cloves, the garlic, carrots, peppercorns, juniper berries (if using), herbs and wine. Close the bag and leave to marinate in the refrigerator for 2 days, turning the meat occasionally.

Transfer the lamb to a roasting pan. Strain the marinade and reserve.

Rub the lamb with the oil and sprinkle with a little salt and pepper. Roast in a preheated hot oven, 230°C (450°F), Gas Mark 8, for 15 minutes, then reduce the heat to moderate, 180°C (350°F), Gas Mark 4. Continue roasting for 1½ hours or until the lamb is cooked to your liking.

Meanwhile, boil the marinade until reduced to 300 ml (½ pint).

Melt the butter in another pan. Add the shallots and fry until softened. Add the flour and cook, stirring, for 2 minutes. Gradually stir in the reduced marinade and consommé. Bring to the boil, stirring, and simmer until thickened. Add the chopped parsley and adjust the seasoning. Serve this sauce with the lamb. Garnish with the herbs.

Serves 6 to 8

Roast Turkey with Almond Stuffing

1 x 5-6 kg (10-12 lb) oven-ready turkey
4 streaky bacon rashers
150 ml (¼ pint) turkey giblet or chicken stock
parsley sprigs to garnish
STUFFING:
125 g (4 oz) butter
2 onions, finely chopped
250 g (8 oz) smoked ham, minced
125 g (4 oz) fresh breadcrumbs
4 tablespoons chopped parsley
½ teaspoon dried thyme
4 tablespoons dry red wine
2 eggs
75 g (3 oz) blanched almonds; chopped
salt and pepper

Prepare the stuffing first. Melt the butter in a frying pan. Add the onions and fry until softened. Remove from the heat and stir in the ham and breadcrumbs, followed by the remaining stuffing ingredients with salt and pepper to taste.

Wipe the turkey inside and out. Put the stuffing into the neck cavity, then secure with skewers or trussing needle and strong thread. Place the turkey in a roasting pan. Put the bacon rashers over the breast. Cover with foil and roast in a preheated moderate oven, 160°C (325°F), Gas Mark 3, for 3½ hours. Turn the turkey from time to time and baste with the stock.

Remove the foil and bacon and continue roasting for 15 to 30 minutes or until the turkey is cooked through and the breast is golden brown.

Transfer the turkey to a warmed serving platter and untruss. Garnish with parsley sprigs and serve with the traditional accompaniments: bacon rolls, chipolata sausages, roast potatoes, and gravy made from the pan juices.

Serves 10 to 12

Christmas Pudding

250 g (8 oz) self-raising flour
1 teaspoon salt
2 teaspoons grated nutmeg
½ teaspoon ground cinnamon
½ teaspoon ground cloves
500 g (1 lb) light brown sugar
350 g (12 oz) fresh breadcrumbs
350 g (12 oz) shredded beef suet
2 kg (4½ lb) mixed dried fruit (sultanas, raisins, currants)
50 g (2 oz) flaked blanched almonds
125 g (4 oz) glacé cherries, halved
1 large cooking apple, peeled, cored and grated
grated rind and juice of 1 large orange
6 eggs
150 ml (¼ pint) stout
3 tablespoons brandy to serve

Sift the flour, salt and spices into a large bowl. Add the sugar, breadcrumbs, suet, fruit, almonds and glacé cherries and mix well.

Combine the apple, orange rind and juice, eggs and stout and add to the dry ingredients. Fold together thoroughly. Divide the mixture between two 1.25 kg (2½ lb) pudding basins, remembering to tuck a coin wrapped in greaseproof paper into each pudding. Cover with greased greaseproof paper and foil, making a pleat in the centre to allow the pudding to expand, and tie on securely with string.

Place each pudding basin in a large saucepan, containing boiling water to reach two-thirds up the sides of the basins. Cook for 5 hours, adding more boiling water as necessary.

Remove the puddings, allow to cool then cover with fresh greaseproof paper and foil. Store in a cool dry place until required.

To serve, boil or steam the puddings for a further 3 hours. Turn out onto a warmed dish and decorate with a sprig of holly. Warm the brandy, pour over the pudding and set alight. Serve flaming, with brandy butter or rum sauce.

Makes 2 large puddings

Cranberry Nut Bread

250 g (8 oz) plain flour
250 g (8 oz) caster sugar
1½ teaspoons baking powder
½ teaspoon bicarbonate of soda
1 teaspoon salt
50 g (2 oz) butter
1 tablespoon grated orange rind
120 ml (4 fl oz) orange juice
1 egg, beaten
50 g (2 oz) walnuts, chopped
250 g (8 oz) fresh cranberries, chopped

Sift the flour, sugar, baking powder, soda and salt into a mixing bowl. Rub in the butter thoroughly, then beat in the orange rind and juice and egg. Fold in the nuts and cranberries.

Pour the batter into a greased 1 kg (2 lb) loaf tin. Bake in a preheated moderate oven, 180°C (350°F), Gas Mark 4, for 1 hour or until a skewer inserted into the centre comes out clean. Cool in the tin.

Makes one 1 kg (2 lb) tea loaf

Christmas Date Wreath

125 g (4 oz) sugar
1 tablespoon plain flour
1 teaspoon baking powder
2 eggs, separated
1 teaspoon vanilla essence
175 g (6 oz) stoned dates, finely chopped
125 g (4 oz) mixed nuts (walnuts, almonds, etc.), finely chopped
5 tablespoons medium sherry
125 g (4 oz) icing sugar
2-3 tablespoons warm water
glacé cherries and candied angelica to decorate

Beat together the sugar, flour, baking powder, egg yolks and vanilla until well blended and fluffy. Stir in the dates and nuts. Beat the egg whites until stiff and fold in. Spoon into a greased decorative 23 cm (9 inch) ring mould. Bake in a preheated moderate oven, 180°C (350°F), Gas Mark 4, for 30 minutes or until the cake springs back when lightly pressed.

Remove from the oven and sprinkle with 4 tablespoons of the sherry. Leave to cool.

Mix the icing sugar with the rest of the sherry and enough warm water to make a thin icing. Remove the cake carefully from the mould and place on a serving platter. Drizzle over the icing, allowing it to run down the sides. Decorate with glacé cherries and angelica and leave until set. Serve with whipped cream.
Serves 6 to 8

INDEX

Acknowledgments

Photography by Paul Williams
Food prepared by Heather Lambert

Designed by Astrid Publishing Consultants Ltd
The publishers would like to thank
Habitat Limited and Le Creuset for the
loan of accessories for photography.